You Be The Judge

(Is Christianity True?)

by Don Stewart

AusAmerica Publishers
Box 6486
Orange, California 92613

You Be The Judge
by Don Stewart

Published by
AusAmerica Publishers
Box 6486
Orange, California 92613

© 1990 Don Stewart

ISBN 1-877825-02-6
(previously published by
Here's Life Publishers ISBN 0-89840-055-4).

Printed in the United States of America

Scripture quotations are taken from the
New King James Bible.

Second Printing January 1993

CONTENTS

Part III
WEIGHING THE EVIDENCE

Part IV
THE VERDICT

DEDICATION

This book is dedicated to my wonderful mother who encouraged me to "study the Scriptures" to see if they were true.

INTRODUCTION

If you were called to pass judgment in court do you feel confident that you could render a fair and just verdict? Judges are committed to make decisions. They have pledged to make fair decisions which affect people and society in important ways. They don't have the luxury of saying, "I don't feel like giving an opinion on the matter right now. I'm not really interested in the subject." Instead, judges work within the system to express their best opinions on the evidence available.

What do judges have to do with a book about God? Well, each thinking person is a "judge" many times a day—we all make numerous decisions that we believe are right, based upon the best available evidence. We cannot live without making decisions, even though we sometimes try to avoid them. Putting off a decision even becomes a decision in itself. If there is a God, who has revealed Himself to mankind through the person of Jesus Christ, then a decision about Him is the most important decision you, as "judge," can ever make!

Maybe you think you're not interested, or do not have the time to make a decision. But especially in this case, no decision becomes a decision of rejection through default.

If Jesus Christ is whom He claimed to be, none of us can afford to ignore His claims or refuse to judge the evidence.

Together in this book we will examine the claims of Jesus Christ. Is He the Lord of the universe? Anything less than this makes Christianity a farce.

You be the judge.

Setting The Record Straight

The Bible Encourages People to Think

Unfortunately, many people today hold the view that becoming a Christian means sacrificing one's intellect, assassinating one's brains. Nothing could be further from the truth. If the God of the Bible is the God of truth, then no truth, whether from logic, science, history, or any other place will contradict God and His revelation. In fact, we find that the God of the Bible affirms the importance of truth and rationality. Jesus said, "You shall love the Lord your God with all your heart, with all your soul, and with all your mind" (Matthew 22:37).

We are supposed to use our minds to think, to weigh the issues. The Apostle Paul wrote, "Test all things; hold fast what is good" (1 Thessalonians 5:21).

How do we test things? We have to use our mind. Another New Testament writer put it this way, "Beloved, do not believe every spirit, but test the spirits, whether they are of God" (1 John 4:1).

The Bible assumes that people should and do use their minds to make wise decisions: "So when Jesus saw that he answered wisely, He said to him, 'You are not far from the kingdom of God' " (Mark 12:34). In this case, wisdom or intelligence is equated with knowing God.

The Apostle Paul wrote to the church at Corinth, "I speak as to wise men; judge for yourselves what I say" (1 Corinthians 10:15).

A key verse of the New Testament with regard to defending the faith is 1 Peter 3:15: "But sanctify the Lord God in your hearts, and always be ready to give a defense to everyone who asks you a reason for the hope that is in you, with meekness and fear" (1 Peter 3:15).

This verse commands Christians to know what they believe about God and why they believe it. The Bible affirms the importance of thinking straight about all matters.

All Religions Are Not The Same

"Why make such a big fuss about Jesus Christ and Christianity? All religions teach the same thing." This is a common belief among many people today. They wonder why Christians make a big issue out of Jesus Christ when He, they say, was basically saying the same thing as Buddha, Confucius, Muhammad and many other religious leaders.

After one of my lectures in Southern California, a Muslim approached me with the same complaint. He said all religions were the same and I should not emphasize Jesus Christ and Christianity as the only way. He illustrated his point by telling me this story, "Suppose you take ten people, blindfold them, then lead them to your backyard where you have an elephant. You have each one touch a different part of the elephant without telling them what it is they are touching. One touches the tail, one the trunk, and so on. You then lead them all back inside your house, take off their blindfolds and ask them to describe what they have touched. Would their descriptions agree?"

I saw where his illustration was heading, but went along anyway. I said, "No, they would not agree because they were all describing a different part of the elephant. The man who felt the trunk would not give the same description as the man who touched the tail."

The Muslim was triumphant. "You see, they all touched the same thing an elephant but they all described it differently. Isn't this how it is when it comes to the subject of God? Don't all religions describe the same God, yet in different terms, as the ten people described the same elephant, yet they touched a different part of it?"

I replied, "Sir, you cannot identify God with the elephant. The Muslims, Buddhists, Christians and other religious groups cannot all be experiencing the same God because their definitions of God are contradictory.

For example, Buddhism does not separate God from His creation, they are one in the same. However Christianity believes and teaches that God is personal, He is not the same essence as His creation but has a separate existence.

The idea this person holds, that all religions are basically the same, does not fit the facts. Some religions believe in only one God while others worship many gods. Since the various religions teach different and contradictory things about God, they cannot all be true at the same time. They can all be wrong, but they cannot all be true. It is impossible for God to be personal and impersonal at the same time, to be all-powerful and limited, etc.

The claims of Christ

Hence, to say that all religions are the same shows a lack of understanding of these religions. Some of them, including Christianity, claim their way is the "only way." Jesus said, "I am the way, the truth, and the life. No one comes to the Father except through Me" (John 14:6).

This sounds pretty exclusive. According to Jesus, no one can get to God except through Him. Any religion which teaches another way to know God is at that point incorrect. This claim of Jesus does not in and of itself make it true, but it does rule out the possibility of Christianity being compatible with other religions.

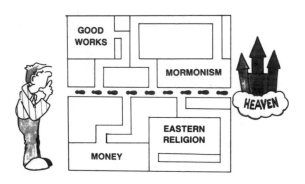

Truth Is Absolute

"I'm glad Christianity has helped you, but don't tell me I have to believe it. What's true for you might not be true for me!"

Sound familiar? Speaking around the world, I hear this frequently. Once I was speaking to a particular religious group that believed all religions have truth in them and that no *one* religion is the only way. When I gave my testimony of how Jesus Christ changed my life and gave me a purpose for living, they were happy for me. However, when I told them that Jesus was not only the truth for me, but also the truth for them, they immediately became hostile. They said what was important was belief, not what you believe in—whether it be Jesus, another religion or even yourself.

Christianity was true for me but not for them.

The Bible teaches just the opposite. It is the object of faith, Jesus Christ, and not faith itself, that is stressed. As far as the Bible is concerned, correct belief is crucial. The Scriptures teach that right belief consists of several things.

First, faith must be in God but not just any god. Faith must be placed in the God of the Bible.

Second, faith must be placed in God's Son, Jesus Christ. This is the only way to have a personal relationship with God. The Bible says, "But as many as received Him, to them He gave the right to become children of God, even to those who believe in His name" (John 1:12).

In addition, faith is more than mere mental assent. It consists of trusting Christ as one's personal Savior. The mere intellectual understanding that Christ is the Son of God is not the issue. The biblical writer James commented on ineffective, intellectual assent, comparing it to the ineffectual belief of demons:

"You believe that there is one God. You do well. Even the demons believe—and tremble" (James 2:19).

According to the Bible, unless someone places his trust in God's Son, Jesus Christ, he cannot receive God's forgiveness or enter into a personal relationship with Him. It does matter what you believe.

What Is The Christian Message?

Part of preparing our "case" for Jesus
Christ to present to the "court" of the world
is for us to define the Christian message
itself. Before one can weigh the pros and
cons about Christianity he must first
understand what it is and what it is saying.
The message of the Christian faith can be
stated simply in the following terms:

In the beginning the infinite, personal,
and loving God created man in His own
image (part of that image is that man is
personal, and has free will, and can make
decisions). Using that decision-making
ability, mankind chose to sever his perfect
relationship with God. This brought
physical and spiritual death into the world.

Broken Relationships

The relationship between God and man
was broken. No longer could man approach
God directly. The harmony between man
and the natural world was broken.
Mankind, created with authority over
nature, became subject to the harsh ways of
nature and was often its victim. The
harmony which was designed by God to be
among all mankind was destroyed.
Tension, disagreement, war, and even death
became the standard results of men and
women interacting. Man even became his
own enemy. Without harmony between the
individual and God, and with the resultant
disharmony throughout the rest of his
relationships, man was not even happy

with himself. Isolated, lonely, incomplete, less than the best for which he was designed, mankind needed a restoration in his relationship with God.

Restoration Through Christ

The restoration was accomplished when God became a man in the person of Jesus Christ. The God-man willingly died for the sins of each person, past, present, and future and made the way clear for restoration and perfect order: a renewed relationship between man and God and harmony in the world. All that remains is for individuals to receive, by faith, the work of God through the sacrifice of Jesus Christ. They will then enter into eternal life prepared for all who believe.

This is a brief summary of the message of the Bible. As we can see, however, the message of the Bible is not primarily a code of ethics, a cultural heritage, a system of laws, or a collection of a record of events. The message has its origin and focal point in a person: the Lord from heaven, Jesus Christ our Savior.

Christianity Is A Person

The great religions of the world consist mainly of sets of laws and teachings that must be obeyed. For Muslims it is found in the Koran, for Buddhists in the teaching of Buddha, and for Confucianists, it is contained in the wisdom of Confucius.

However, Christianity is a faith based upon a person rather than a set of teachings. At its center is Jesus Christ who reveals and represents God. He is the only figure in history who proved He was God in human flesh. The issue, therefore, in Christianity is not so much what Jesus taught but whom He claimed to be. The Bible says the way you view Him and relate to Him will determine your eternal destiny.

"He who believes in the Son has everlasting life; and he who does not believe the Son shall not see life, but the wrath of God abides on him" (John 3:36).

Simon Peter said, "Nor is there salvation in any other, for there is no other name under heaven given among men by which we must be saved" (Acts 4:12).

The claims of Christ

The Bible makes it clear that Jesus Christ claimed to be God in human flesh. Those claims must be dealt with. One of the following four possibilities must fit the evidence:

(1) Jesus never made the claims about Himself. His disciples, who wrote the New Testament long after His death, exaggerated His claims.

(2) Jesus was not God, but He made the claim to be God. He knew the claims were not true, yet He made them anyway.

(3) Jesus was not God, but He made the claims truly believing He was God.

(4) Jesus made the claims about Himself, and He was whom He claimed to be: the Lord of the universe.

A Legend?

The first possibility, that Jesus never made the claims about Himself recorded in the New Testament, does not square with the facts. The twenty-seven books of the New Testament were all written by either eyewitnesses or those who recorded eyewitness testimony. There was simply not enough time for legends about Him to snowball to the place where all accounts had Him claiming to be God. The New Testament gives unanimous testimony that Jesus made these claims. The first books were written within twenty-five years of His death, not nearly enough time for people to assume that Jesus claimed to be God had He not made the claims. The importance of eyewitness testimony was not lost on the New Testament writers who repeatedly appealed to first-hand evidence to substantiate their assertions. For example, one of Jesus' disciples, John, wrote, "That which was from the beginning, which we have heard, which we have seen with our eyes, which we have looked upon, and our hands have handled, concerning the Word of life—the life was manifested, and we have seen, and bear witness, and declare to you that eternal life which was with the Father and was manifested to us" (1 John 1:1-2).

One of the gospel writers, Luke, based the truthfulness of his entire book on its eyewitness sources:

"Inasmuch as many have taken in hand to set in order a narrative of those things which are most surely believed among us, just as those who from the beginning were eyewitnesses and ministers of the word delivered them to us, it seemed good to me also, having had perfect understanding of all things from the very first, to write to you an orderly account, most excellent Theophilus, that you may know the certainty of those things in which you were instructed" (Luke 1:1-4).

Biblical and historical scholar F. F. Bruce has well summarized the importance of the eyewitness testimony: "The earliest preachers of the gospel knew the value of . . . first-hand testimony, and appealed to it time and time again. 'We are witnesses of these things,' was their constant and confident assertion. And it can have been

by no means so easy as some writers seem
to think to invent words and deeds of Jesus
in those early years, when so many of His
disciples were about, who could remember
what had and had not happened . . .

"And it was not only friendly
eyewitnesses that the early preachers had
to reckon with; there were others . . .
conversant with the main facts of the
ministry and death of Jesus. The disciples
could not afford to risk inaccuracies (not to
speak of willful manipulation of the facts),
which would at once be exposed by those
who would be only too glad to do so . . . one
of the strongpoints in the   original
apostolic preaching is the confident appeal
to the knowledge of the hearers; they not
only said, 'We are witnesses of these things,'
but also, 'As you yourselves know' (Acts
2:22). Had there been any tendency to depart
from the facts in any material respect, the
possible presence of hostile witnesses in the
audience would have served as a further
corrective" (F. F. Bruce, *The New Testament
Documents: Are They Reliable?*, Downers
Grove, IL: InterVarsity Press, 1964 p. 33, 44-
46).

Because of the early dates of composition
and circulation of the New Testament
books and the evidential and substantiated
nature of those books, it is impossible that
Jesus never made the unique claims for
which Christianity stands: His sacrifice on
the cross, His forgiveness of sin, His
resurrection from the dead, and His second
coming.

A Lie?

The second possibility is that Jesus made the claims about Himself, yet knew they were not true. This view identifies Jesus as a liar. We shall see that it contradicts everything that we know about Him. There is absolutely no evidence that Jesus ever lied about anything. On the contrary, His teachings and actions were consistently truthful and emphasized the essential importance of truth. Therefore, to say that He lied about the very purpose of His coming is completely inconsistent.

Furthermore, a liar who suffers crucifixion for a lie may be a clever actor, but he certainly doesn't appear very smart! To lie for personal gain makes sense in a sinful world and there are many political and even religious leaders who lie as a means to a personally advantageous end. If Jesus were such a liar, we should be able to see at least some personal advantage which would come from His false claims to be God in the flesh. What personal advantage is there to being pressured night and day to perform miracles and healings? What personal advantage is there in denying one's own home and comforts to become a poor, traveling preacher with few friends and "nowhere to lay His head?" What personal advantage is there to losing one's life in a horrible and tortured way as the mortal blow to the movement one has worked so hard to build?

The evidence indicates that Jesus Christ did not deliberately lie about who He was or why He came.

A Delusion?

The third possibility is that Jesus believed Himself to be God in human flesh, while in actuality He was not. This grand delusion could be held only by someone insane. However, the same Jesus, whom some claim was insane when He talked of His identity, is also lauded the world over for His practical teaching and accurate concepts concerning mental and spiritual health and happiness.

The well-respected church historian of the last century, Philip Schaff, remarked, "Is such an intellect—clear as the sky, bracing as the mountain air, sharp and penetrating as a sword, thoroughly healthy and vigorous, always ready and always self-possessed—liable to a radical and most serious delusion concerning His own character and mission? Preposterous imagination!" (Philip Schaff, *The Person of Christ*, New York, NY: American Tract Society, 1913, p. 97, 98).

Christian writer and literary scholar C. S. Lewis wrote, "The historical difficulty of giving for the life, saying and influence of Jesus any explanation that is not harder than the Christian explanation is very great. The discrepancy between the depth and sanity of His moral teaching and the rampant megalomania which must lie behind His theological teaching unless He is indeed God has never been satisfactorily explained" (C.S. Lewis, *Miracles: A Preliminary Study*, New York, NY: The Macmillan Company, 1947, p. 113).

The Truth?

There is one final possibility: Jesus made these claims about Himself and His claims were true—He is God Almighty. If this is the case, then each human being, created in His image, must judge and decide either (1) to accept Him as Savior and Lord, or (2) to reject Him and His gift of eternal life and peace with God. The issue is clear: Jesus is not merely another religious leader who gave the world a nice set of teachings. He did claim to be our "God and Savior." He was not a bold-faced liar. He was not insane. C. S. Lewis says, "I am trying here to prevent anyone saying the really foolish thing that people often say about Him: 'I'm ready to accept Jesus as a great moral teacher, but I don't accept His claim to be God.' That is the one thing we must not say. A man who was merely a man and said the sort of things Jesus said would not be a great moral teacher. He would either be a lunatic—on a level with the man who says he is a poached egg—or else he would be the Devil of Hell. You must make your choice. Either this man was, and is, the Son of God: or else a madman or something worse" (C. S. Lewis, *Mere Christianity*, New York, NY: Macmillan Company, 1952, pp. 40,41).

Jesus Christ is either Lord of all or not Lord at all. If He is Lord of all then we should expect to find sufficient evidence to back up His claim. In the next section we will examine some of the evidence.

The Facts Of The Case

The Christian Faith is Based Upon Fact

Christianity is different from any other religion. It can point to historical evidence to back up its claims while other religions cannot. Other religions appeal to personal experience as their only validation. They are unable to refer to any objective criteria or tangible evidence to verify their claims.

This was illustrated graphically by an encounter I had some years ago. I had just come out of a supermarket when I was greeted by a member of the International Society of Krishna Consciousness (Hare Krishnas). I asked her why she believed her religion was true. Her answer: "Because ever since I converted, my life has been changed for the better. It must be true!"

I said to her, "Ever since I've been a Christian, my life has been changed for the better too, so I know my faith is true. My testimony about Christianity appears to have cancelled out yours about Krishna Consciousness. Are there any objective facts you can give me to validate your belief?" She paused for a long while, shrugged her shoulders and said, "If you'd just try it for yourself, you'd see, I can't explain it to you."

After I explained the evidence for Jesus Christ with her for a few more minutes, she left. I hadn't walked twenty-five feet when a man came up to me and said, "Please buy my magazine. It answers the lifes deepest questions: who are you, why you're here, where you will go after death." I thought he was another Hare Krishna devotee and so I said, "No thanks, I have already talked to your friend over there." He responded, "I'm not with her. She's in darkness. Muhammad is God's prophet!"

I asked the Muslim the same question I had asked before: "Why do you believe your way is true?" He had the same general answer: "Muhammad must have been right. Since I've started serving Allah, my life has changed drastically for the better." Of course, I answered the same way I had with the Krishnaite: "Ever since I trusted Jesus Christ for my salvation, my life has improved. In fact, the Krishna woman said Krishna devotion changed her life. What can you tell me to show me I'm wrong and she's wrong but you're right?"

His pause was as long as hers had been. "Well, I guess I can't really satisfy you but I know the only God is Allah and his prophet is Muhammad because I believe it and feel it." I again had an opportunity to present him with the valid claims of Christ. Coincidentally, the next day a Mormon confronted me who argued for his faith the same way as the Muslim and the Hare Krishna lady. I was able to use what I said to them as examples to him.

Here were three different people: one in Krishna Consciousness, a Muslim, and a Mormon. They all claimed to have "the truth." We know they could not all have been right since each of the three religious systems contradicted each other (and Christianity too). Each of them had an experience which was supposed to validate their beliefs. Yet apart from that they had nothing factual or objective which could substantiate their religious claims. I, as a Christian, have also had an experience that expresses the truth of my faith. Four different people with four different experiences each claiming to know the truth. An agnostic observer would have asked: "How do I know whom to believe? Or should I believe any of them?" Only the Christian can answer that his faith can be tested objectively. The person in whom he trusts, Jesus Christ, is worthy of that trust. Jesus can meet any reasonable test put to Him and His claims as revealed in the Bible. We will look at that validation in the following pages.

THE BIBLE

The Bible claims to be God's Word: "All Scripture is given by inspiration of God, and is profitable for doctrine, for reproof, for correction, for instruction in righteousness" (2 Timothy 3:16).

"For prophecy never came by the will of man, but holy men of God spoke as they were moved by the Holy Spirit" (2 Peter 1:21).

Over 2000 times in the Scriptures we encounter such phrases as "God said," "The word of the Lord came unto Moses," etc. Clearly the Bible portrays itself as God's Word. However, claiming to be God's Word does not make it such. There must be an objective way to test such a claim.

Accurate Transmission

The Bible has been transmitted accurately throughout the centuries since it was composed. The text of the Bible is the same today as when it was originally written. Centuries of copying and distribution around the world have not marred its message. The evidence of its preservation is overwhelming.

We have three types of evidence available to reconstruct the New Testament text. These are the Greek manuscripts, the early versions in which the New Testament was translated and the writings of the early Christians called the Church fathers.

The books of the New Testament were originally written in Greek. There are about 5,500 copies of handwritten Greek manuscripts in existence that date before the invention of the printing press. These manuscripts contain all or part of the New Testament text. Although we do not possess the originals, copies exist from a very early date.

The New Testament was written from about A.D. 50 to A.D. 90. The earliest manuscript fragment dates from about A.D. 120. There are about 50 other manuscript fragments that were written within 150-200 years from the time of the original.

There are two major manuscripts, Codex Vaticanus (A.D. 325) and Codex Sinaiticus, a complete copy (A.D. 350), that date within 250 years of the time of the composition of the New Testament.

Most ancient writings have a long time span from the time they were originally written to the earliest existing manuscript. For example, there is a 1,550 year gap between the time the Latin poet Catullus wrote and the oldest existing manuscript to reconstruct his text. Caesar's *The Gallic Wars* has a one thousand year gap from the time of the original and the earliest existing manuscript copy. The earliest complete copy of Homer's *Illiad* that has survived was written 2,200 years after the original. Hence, the New Testament is much closer in the time span from the original writing to the earliest existing copy than the writers of the Greek and Latin classics.

In addition, the 5,500 Greek manuscript copies are far and away the most we have of any ancient work. Many writings from the ancient world have only a few surviving manuscripts to reconstruct the text (Catullus-3 copies, Herodotus-8 copies). While other ancient works count their manuscripts in the handfuls, the New Testament numbers its manuscripts in the thousands.

The New Testament not only has more manuscripts and a shorter time interval than other ancient works, it was also translated into other languages at a very early date. Translating a document from one language to another was something rare in the ancient world. The number of manuscripts of the translations (or versions), copied before the invention of the printing press, is in excess of 18,000. This is another helpful factor in the reconstruction of the New Testament's text.

Furthermore, the entire New Testament text could be reconstructed within 250 years of its writing without the aid of either the Greek manuscripts or the early versions. This could be accomplished by examining the writings of the early Christians known as the Church fathers. In personal letters, diaries, commentaries,

etc. these men quote the biblical text
providing us with another testimony of
how the text read at their time. At the end
of the last century John Burgon, a biblical
scholar, catalogued more than 86,000
quotations of the New Testament by early
Christian writers living before A.D. 325.
Hence, we see that there is much more
evidence for the New Testament's
reliability than any other writings of the
classical authors of the ancient world.

F. F. Bruce, an authority on the subject,
came to the obvious conclusion: "The
evidence for our New Testament writing is
ever so much greater than the evidence
for many writings of classical authors,
the authenticity of which no one dreams of
questioning . . . And if the New Testament
were a collection of secular writings, their
authenticity would generally be regarded
as beyond all doubt" (F. F. Bruce, *The New
Testament Documents: Are They Reliable?*
Downers Grove: IL: InterVarsity Press
p. 124).

We conclude with the statement of Sir
Frederic Kenyon, the former director and
principal librarian of the British Museum
for fifty years. He was one of the foremost
experts on ancient manuscripts and their
authority. Shortly before his death, he
wrote concerning the New Testament: "The
interval between the dates of the original
composition (of the New Testament) and the
earliest extant evidence becomes so small
as to be in fact negligible, and the last
foundation for any doubt that the

Scriptures have come down to us as they were written has now been removed. Both the authenticity and the general integrity of the books of the New Testament may be regarded as finally established" (Sir Frederic Kenyon, *The Bible and Archaeology*, New York, NY: Harper and Row, Publishers, 1940, pp. 288-289).

The text of the New Testament has been transmitted to us in a most reliable manner. The text has *not* been changed. It says the same thing today as when originally composed.

Reliable History

The Bible is not just a religious record. It is an historical document and has been proven time and again to be historically reliable. The Scriptures give an accurate account of people, places and events of the past. Nelson Glueck, a world famous archaeologist, concluded the following after a lifetime of study on the Bible and its history as it relates to archaeology:

"It may be stated categorically that no archaeological discovery has ever controverted a biblical reference" (Nelson Glueck, *Rivers in the Desert: History of Negev*, Philadelphia, PA: Jewish Pub. Society of America, 1969, p. 31).

The philosophically based higher criticism of the nineteenth century did much to cast doubt on the historical reliability of the Bible. Careful on-site archaeological investigation during the last hundred years has vindicated the absolute trustworthiness of Scripture.

The biblical expert, Sir Frederic Kenyon, concluded, "It is therefore legitimate to say that, in respect to that part of the Old Testament against which the disintegrating criticism of the last half of the nineteenth century was directed, the evidence of archaeology has been to reestablish its authority, and likewise to augment its value by rendering it more intelligible through a fuller knowledge of its background and setting. Archaeology has not yet said its last word; but the results already achieved confirm what faith would suggest, that the Bible can do nothing but gain from an increase of knowledge" (Sir Frederic Kenyon, *The Bible and*

Archaeology, New York, NY: Harper and Row, Publishers, 1940, p. 279).

Sir William Ramsay was one of the greatest archaeologists who has ever lived. His career in archaeology was influenced by his studies in destructive higher criticism of the Bible. He believed he would be unable to trust the New Testament as an historical record. When he later turned to the historical references within the New Testament, he found it remarkably accurate and essential to his continued archaeological research. He wrote, "Great historians are the rarest of writers . . . I will venture to add one to the number of critics, by stating in the following chapters reasons for placing the author of Acts among the historians of the first rank. The first and the essential quality of the great historian is truth. What he says must be trustworthy . . . Our hypothesis is that Acts was written by a great historian" (Sir William Ramsay, *St. Paul the Traveler and the Roman Citizen*, Grand Rapids, MI: Baker Book House, 1897 (1962 reprint), pp. 2-4, 14).

There is an abundance of confirmation of the historicity of the Bible. The above is a brief testimonial to its accuracy.

THE CASE PROVED BY PROPHECY

One of the strongest reasons for accepting the trustworthiness of the Bible is predictive prophecy. Before certain events took place, the Bible predicted they would occur so that people would not doubt the fact of God's existence or His control over history. The following verses state the purpose of prophecy: "Remember the former things of old, for I am God, and there is no other; I am God, and there is none like Me, declaring the end from the beginning, and from ancient times things that are not yet done" (Isaiah 46:9,10). "I have declared the former things from the beginning; they went forth from My mouth, and I caused them to hear it. Suddenly I did them, and they came to pass . . . even from the beginning I have declared it to you . . . lest you should say, 'My idol has done them, and my carved image and my molded image have commanded them'" (Isaiah 48:3,5).

These verses are quite revealing. We are told that God tells us the end from the beginning, things that have not yet transpired, so that when they do happen, we will know that God exists and there is none like Him.

An Example of Fulfilled Prophecy

One example of fulfilled prophecy is recorded in Isaiah 44:28-45:1. The prophet Isaiah, writing about 700 B.C. names Cyrus as the one who will say to the destroyed city of Jerusalem that it shall be rebuilt and the foundation of the temple shall be laid. What is amazing about this prophecy is that at the time of Isaiah's writing, the city was not yet destroyed and the temple was still standing. It was some 100 years after this prediction that the city and temple were destroyed by King Nebuchadnezzar of Babylon.

After Jerusalem was taken captive by the Babylonians, it was conquered by the Persians in 539 B.C. It was shortly after this that a Persian king named Cyrus gave the decree to rebuild the city and temple. This occurred over 160 years after the prophecy of Isaiah.

Amazing as it is, this is not an isolated case. There are literally hundreds of predictions of future events in the Bible that have now been fulfilled.

Objections to Predictive Prophecy

When Christians point to predictive prophecy to demonstrate the existence of God, the following objections are usually brought up:

1.   Others have done the same thing.

One common objection is that other people and other religions have the same thing as the Bible in the area of prophecy. People point to Jeane Dixon, Nostradamus, and other "prophets" to prove their point. However, there is a fundamental difference between these "seers" and the prophets and prophecies.

The Bible clearly defines a true prophet of God: "I will raise up for them a Prophet like you from among their brethren, and will put My words in His mouth, and He shall speak to them all that I command Him. And it shall be that whoever will not hear My words, which he speaks in My name, I will require it of him. But the prophet who presumes to speak a word in My name, which I have not commanded him to speak, or who speaks in the name of other gods, that prophet shall die. And if you say in your heart, 'How shall we know the word which the Lord has not spoken?'— when a prophet speaks in the name of the Lord, if the thing does not happen or come to pass, that is the thing which the Lord has spoken; the prophet has spoken it presumptuously; you shall not be afraid of him" (Deuteronomy 18:18-22).

To be a true prophet a person had to be 100 percent right 100 percent of the time. The biblical prophets always passed this test while none of those listed above, or any others, have ever met the standard. For example, Jeane Dixon falsely predicted;

(1) World War III would begin in 1954;
(2) Red China would be admitted to the United Nations in 1958, yet this did not occur until 1971.
(3) The Vietnam War would end in 1966, yet it did not end until 1975;
(4) On October 19, 1968, she predicted Jacqueline Kennedy was not thinking

about marriage, and the next day Mrs. Kennedy married Aristotle Onassis!

Searching far and wide, through contemporary "prophets" and historical "prophecies," one cannot find any other collection of prophets where each and every prophet was 100 percent right. The biblical prophets did not make mistakes.

2. The prophecies were written after the fact.

A popular objection contends that the prophecies were written after the fact. Certain events took place and then long afterward they were written down as prophecy. This objection has no basis in fact.

For example, the Old Testament, which contained the prophecies of the coming Messiah, was completed in 400 B.C. There is at least a 400-year gap between the time these messianic prophecies first were written down by the time they were fulfilled by Jesus of Nazareth.

3. Too vague.

Another objection is that the prophecies contained in the Bible are too vague. Supposedly they are so general and non-specific that anything that happened could be pointed to as their fulfillment. However, the Scriptures are anything but vague.

The Old Testament messianic prophecies were very specific in predicting the details of the Messiah's coming. The things predicted of Him included the following:

(1) He would be born in Bethlehem (Micah 5:2). No other city in the world would qualify.

(2) Daniel 9:27 says the Messiah would come before the second temple was destroyed (it was destroyed in A.D. 70). Anyone coming on the scene of history after that time would have no biblical right to claim to be the promised Messiah.

(3) He would be born of the line of Abraham (Genesis 22:18); of the line of Isaac (Genesis 21:12); of the line of Jacob (Numbers 24:17); of the tribe of Judah (Genesis 49:10); in the family line of Jesse (Isaiah 11:1); and of the line of David (Jeremiah 23:5).

There are many other specific prophecies written in the Old Testament that Jesus Christ fulfilled perfectly. The biblical prophecies are not vague.

4. The fulfillment was contrived.

Sometimes it is argued that the prophecies given in Scripture were contrived or deliberately fulfilled. For example, Jesus, the skeptic argues, knowing the prophecies of the coming Messiah, purposely fulfilled them to prove He was the promised One. The problem with this view is twofold:

(1) It would involve Jesus in a hoax. He would have had to knowingly and willingly contrive to fulfill these prophecies. This would make Him a deceiver, contrary to everything that we know He taught and lived. It does not fit the facts we know about Jesus.

(2) Many prophecies are beyond human manipulation or fulfillment. One has no control over his place of birth, city of birth, family tree, etc. By the place, city, and time of His birth Jesus fulfilled many prophecies that, humanly speaking, were beyond His control.

5. Fulfillment was coincidental.

It is sometimes argued that the prophecies fulfilled from Scripture were fulfilled coincidentally. However, this does not square with the facts. The possibility of coincidence is ruled out by an examination of the evidence. Peter Stoner in his book *Science Speaks* shows that the modern science of probability, when applied to Scripture, rules out coincidence. He does so by examining only eight of the prophecies Jesus fulfilled at His first coming:

"We find that the chance that any man might have lived down to the present time and fulfilled all eight prophecies is 1 in 10^{17} . . . This is illustrated by taking 10^{17} silver dollars and laying them on the face of Texas. They will cover all of the state two feet deep. Now mark one of these silver dollars and stir the whole mass thoroughly, all over the state. Blindfold a man and tell him he can travel as far as he wishes, but he must pick up one silver dollar and say that this is the right one. What chance would he have of getting the right one? Just the same chance that the prophets would have had of writing these eight prophecies and having them all come true in any one man, from their day to the present time, provided they wrote them in their own wisdom.

"Now these prophecies were either given by inspiration of God or the prophets just wrote them as they thought they should be. In such a case the prophets had just one chance in 10^{17} of being absolute" (Peter W. Stoner and Robert C. Newman, *Science Speaks,* Chicago, IL: Moody Press, 1976, pp. 106-112).

Conclusion

When the evidence is considered for predictive prophecy the verdict becomes clear. The biblical prophets were able to predict future events accurately and in detail. There is no possible way that this could be attributed to coincidence or lucky guessing. The prophets demonstrate that it was God Himself who inspired them and gave them insight into the future.

THE RESURRECTION WITNESS

The resurrection of Jesus Christ is unique to Christianity: No other religious figure has ever predicted his own resurrection, then accomplished it. All other religions are based on a founder in the past whose religion is his only legacy. Christianity is based on the eternal and living Christ: the Son of God. His resurrection is the testimonial that He is the one whom He claimed to be.

Not An Afterthought

The resurrection was in the eternal plan of God. It was not an afterthought. Jesus' death and resurrection were predicted in the Old Testament. The crucifixion and resurrection did not take Him by surprise:

"Now it came to pass, when Jesus had finished all these sayings, that He said to His disciples, 'You know that after two days is the Passover, and the Son of Man will be delivered up to be crucified.' Then the chief priests, the scribes, and the elders of the people assembled at the palace of the high priest, who was called Caiaphas, and plotted to take Jesus by trickery and kill Him. But they said, 'Not during the feast, lest there be an uproar among the people" (Matthew 26:1-5).

The Apostle Peter, speaking under inspiration of the Holy Spirit on the day of Pentecost, fifty days after the Passover of Jesus' death, declared: "Men of Israel, hear these words: Jesus of Nazareth, a Man attested by God to you by miracles, wonders, and signs which God did through Him in your midst, as you yourselves also know— Him, being *delivered by the determined counsel and foreknowledge of God*, you have taken by lawless hands, have crucified, and put to death; whom God raised up, having loosed the pains of death, because it was not possible that He should be held by it" (Acts 2:22-24).

Not Too Hard For God

Many object to the resurrection on the grounds that it would be too hard for God to accomplish. Why would it be so hard for the author of life to give life to the dead? The first verse of the Bible says, "In the beginning God created the heavens and the earth" (Genesis 1:1). If God can do that, if He can speak the universe into existence, what's so hard about accomplishing a resurrection? He has already established that He has the power. That's why the Apostle Paul declared, "Why should it be thought incredible by you that God raises the dead?" (Acts 26:8).

The Resurrection Foretold

As one reads the four gospels, he is struck by the fact that Jesus predicted over and over again His betrayal, death, and resurrection. Three years before the resurrection, the following exchange between Him and the Jewish religious leaders occurred:

"So the Jews answered and said to Him, 'What sign do You show to us, since You do these things?' Jesus answered and said to them, 'Destroy this temple, and in three days I will raise it up.' Then the Jews said, 'It has taken forty-six years to build this temple, and will You raise it up in three days?' But He was speaking of the temple of His body" (John 2:18-21).

Especially during the last six months of His earthly life, Jesus emphasized the importance and necessity of His coming crucifixion and the triumph of His coming resurrection.

"From that time Jesus began to show to His disciples that He must go to Jerusalem, and suffer many things from the elders and chief priests and scribes, and be killed, and be raised again the third day" (Matthew 16:21).

Jesus made the amazing claim that He had the power to accomplish the resurrection Himself: "Therefore My Father loves Me, because I lay down My life that I may take it again. No one takes it from Me, but I lay it down of Myself. I have power to lay it down, and I have power to take it again" (John 10:17, 18).

Preparing the Crime Scene

The events leading to the resurrection give evidential testimony of its truthfulness. Jesus' own enemies worked to secure the death and burial scene from any interference from zealous disciples who might attempt to steal Jesus' body and fake a resurrection. Their deliberate care is one of the assurances that the resurrection was not faked. The predictions by Jesus of His resurrection were of such common knowledge that it led the religious rulers to Pontius Pilate to secure the tomb:

"On the next day, which followed the Day of Preparation, the chief priests and Pharisees gathered together to Pilate, saying, 'Sir, we remember, while He was still alive, how that deceiver said, 'After three days I will rise.' Therefore command that the tomb be made secure until the third day, lest His disciples come by night and steal Him away, and say to the people, 'He has risen from the dead.' So the last deception will be worse than the first.' Pilate said to them, 'You have a guard; go your way, make it as secure as you know how" (Matthew 27:62-65).

The precautions taken at the tomb consisted of three things: (1) the stone (2) the Roman seal; and (3) the Roman guard.

The Roman seal was a sign of authentication that the tomb was occupied and that the power and authority of Rome stood behind it. Anyone breaking the seal would suffer the punishment of death. The Roman guard stood as the final obstacle to anyone desiring to remove the body.

These precautions made the religious rulers feel secure that the testimony of Jesus would soon go away. After three and a half years of tracking Him down, they had finally found an opportunity to put Him to death. Now Jesus lay dead in the tomb and His disciples were scattered. They believed they had won.

The First Easter

But the story was not over. The Bible says that early Sunday morning the women came to the tomb to anoint the body of Jesus. They found the stone removed and the body gone. An angel at the tomb asked: "Why do you seek the living among the dead? He is not here, but is risen" (Luke 24:5,6). They went back to tell the other disciples, who at first did not believe. However, they were persuaded to look for themselves, and they also found the tomb empty. This caused them confusion.

The confusion vanished as the resurrected Christ first appeared to Mary Magdalene, then to some other women, and then to the disciples. After being with the disciples forty days Jesus ascended into heaven. Ten days later the disciples publicly proclaimed to all Jerusalem the fact that Jesus had risen from the dead.

Presenting The Case

As we examine the biblical account of the resurrection, there are certain facts that are undisputed and upon which friend and foe alike must agree.

1. Jesus predicted His resurrection.

It was *the* sign that demonstrated He was the one He claimed to be. The reason the religious leaders asked Pontius Pilate for a guard at the tomb is because they were aware that Jesus Himself had predicted His resurrection.

2. The disciples were not prepared for His death.

The disciples were expecting Jesus to conquer the Romans and install Himself as King. To their minds, the Messiah would be the conquering King. The predictions by Jesus of His death were not heeded. When He did die, they were totally unprepared.

3. Jesus was dead and buried.

This is a fact beyond dispute since the eyewitnesses, both friend and foe, testified to it.

4. The tomb was empty

This is yet another undisputed fact. If the tomb had remained occupied, it would have been a simple thing for the Romans and Jews to remove the stone and produce the body. However, they admitted the tomb was empty but tried to explain it by saying the disciples had stolen the body.

5. The disciples testified they had seen the risen Christ.

The disciples of Jesus had certain experiences which they said were with the risen Christ. They claimed to have seen Him alive after His death.

6. The disciples proclaimed the resurrection in Jerusalem.

They did not go to Rome where the evidence would be hard to check, but they proclaimed it in Jerusalem, the very city Jesus was buried.

7. The New Testament writers believed Jesus had risen.

When the New Testament was committed to writing, it was from the perspective that Jesus had risen. All of the New Testament writers believed the resurrection occurred and something led them to that belief. What made them believe?

These facts are not in dispute. We know that Jesus predicted His death and resurrection, that the disciples were not prepared for this, that Jesus was dead and buried, and yet the tomb was empty on Easter morning. The empty tomb did not make them believers; what did was seeing the risen Christ. The disciples proclaimed the resurrection in Jerusalem. And all the New Testament writers believed the resurrection was a reality.

The Case For the Resurrection

1. The appearances.

The main reason the disciples believed in the resurrection of Jesus is that they saw Him alive after He was dead. J. N. D. Anderson, Christian scholar and professor of Islamic studies, said concerning the testimony of the eyewitnesses, "The most drastic way of dismissing the evidence would be to say that these stories were mere fabrications, that they were pure lies. But, so far as I know, not a single critic today would take such an attitude. In fact, it would really be an impossible position. Think of the number of witnesses, over 500. Think of the character of the witnesses, men and women who gave the world the highest ethical teaching it has ever known, and who even on the testimony of their enemies lived it out in their lives. Think of the psychological absurdity of picturing a little band of defeated cowards cowering in an upper room one day and a few days later transformed into a company that no persecution could silence—and then attempting to attribute this dramatic change to nothing more convincing than a miserable fabrication they were trying to foist upon the world. That simply wouldn't make any sense" (J. N. D. Anderson, "The Resurrection of Jesus Christ" in *Christianity Today*, March 29, 1968, pp. 5,6).

Well-known Christian attorney John Warwick Montgomery described the importance of eyewitness testimony of the resurrection: "Note that when the disciples of Jesus proclaimed the resurrection, they did so as eyewitnesses and they did so while people were still alive who had had contact with the events they spoke of. In A.D. 56 Paul wrote that over 500 people had seen the risen Jesus and that most of them were still alive (1 Corinthians 15:6). It passes the bounds of credibility that the early Christians could have manufactured such a tale and then preached it among those who might easily have refuted it simply by producing the body of Jesus" (John

Warwick Montgomery, *History and Christianity*, Downers Grove, IL: InterVarsity Press, 1964, p. 78).

The resurrected Christ appeared to different people over many days in a variety of different places. He appeared to Mary Magdalene (John 20:14); to women returning from the empty tomb (Matthew 28:9,10); to the Apostle Peter the same day (Luke 24:34); to the disciples on the way to Emmaus (Luke 24:13-33); to all of the disciples including Thomas (John 20:26-29); to seven disciples by the Sea of Tiberias (John 21:1 23); to more than 500 believers in Galilee (1 Corinthians 15:6); to James (1 Corinthians 15:7); to the eleven apostles (Matthew 28:16-20; Mark 16:14-20; Luke 24:33-52; Acts 1:3-12); to the Apostle Paul at his conversion (Acts 9:3-6); and finally to the Apostle John on Patmos (Revelation 1:10-19).

2. Lack of an adequate alternative theory.

The lack of a coherent alternative explanation which fits the evidence speaks as loudly as the positive testimony of the believers. All theories that have attempted to explain what happened are inadequate at best (see Alternative Theories below).

3. The changed lives of the disciples.

Something had changed the disciples of Jesus from cowards to martyrs, from frightened individuals to bold proclaimers of the resurrection. It was certainly something more powerful and persuasive than a mere hope, dream, delusion or lie. They said it was because they had seen the risen Christ.

4. The conversion of Saul of Tarsus.

Saul of Tarsus, the greatest antagonist of the Christian faith, was converted and became the Apostle Paul, a great proclaimer of the faith. He testified it was seeing the risen Christ that changed his life.

5. The rise of the Christian church.

Christianity spread faster than any other ancient religion or philosophy, overtaking the Roman empire by the fourth century. Something made it grow this fast—something at least as compelling as a resurrected Christ.

Alternative Theories

If the resurrection did not occur, then some plausible alternative must be brought up to explain what really did happen. However, all theories that attempt to explain away the resurrection are inadequate. These include:

1. The stolen body theory.

The oldest explanation given is that the body of Jesus was stolen by His disciples while the guard was sleeping. Matthew tells us this was the story the bribed Roman guard was to tell, even though they knew it was false: "Now while they were going, behold, some of the guard came into the city and reported to the chief priests all the things that had happened. When they had assembled with the elders and taken counsel, they gave a large sum of money to the soldiers, saying, 'Tell them, His disciples came at night and stole Him away while we slept. And if this comes to the governor's ears, we will appease him and make you secure.' So they took the money and did as they were instructed; and this saying is commonly reported among the Jews until this day" (Matthew 28:11-15).

The stolen body theory is inadequate for the following reasons:

(1) If the guards were asleep, how did they know the disciples stole the body? How can you determine anything that's going on while you are asleep? Couldn't He have risen just as easily while they were asleep without them knowing it?

(2) The stolen body theory would make the disciples liars. Even if they could have gotten past the Roman guard to get to the body, they would have had to live with that lie for the rest of their lives, proclaiming it, suffering for it, dying for it and preaching in direct contradiction to their own knowledge of truth.

The disciples who would have "died for a lie" included Peter (crucified); Andrew (crucified); Matthew (by the sword); James, son of Alphaeus (crucified); Philip (crucified); Simon (crucified); Thaddaeus (killed with arrows); James, brother of Jesus (stoning); Thomas (by a spear); Bartholomew (crucified); and James, son of

Zebedee (crucified). It is one thing to lie; it is quite another thing to die for a lie if you know that its a lie. The disciples sealed their testimony in their own blood.

2. The disciples hallucinated.

Some have argued that the disciples saw something they mistook for Jesus, some type of hallucination or vision. If it were only a hallucination they saw, that would mean the body of Christ was still in the tomb. The authorities could have produced the body, ending any testimony that Jesus had risen. The hallucination theory does not explain the missing body. Furthermore, hallucinations are not collective, but are experienced by individuals. Five hundred people at one time do not have the same hallucination! Hallucinations do not come for just a forty-day period, then suddenly stop. They tend to recur. The testimony of the disciples is that after forty days Jesus ascended into heaven and they saw Him no longer.

Other theories inadequate

In the last two thousand years many other theories have been presented that attempt to give an alternative explanation to the one given in Scripture—namely Christ rose from the dead. None of them are adequate, for they do not fully explain all the different lines of evidence.

The theory that best fits all the facts is that Jesus Christ was alive three days after His death.

The Significance Of The Resurrection

If we concur that the resurrection did take place, then so what? What does it mean? Christ's resurrection means several things.

1. It validates Jesus' claims.

The resurrection demonstrates that Jesus is the one He claimed to be, "And declared to be the Son of God with power, according to the Spirit of holiness, by the resurrection from the dead" (Romans 1:4).

2. It gives us hope for the future.

Because Jesus has risen, we have a hope for something better. Jesus said, "Because I live, you will live also" (John 14:19). This life is not all there is. There is hope beyond the grave.

3. It offers us spiritual life right now.

That life is available right now because Christ has risen. The power of the resurrected Christ is experienced in the life of the believer.

The evidence testifies that Jesus Christ has risen! The only rational explanation for these historical facts is that God raised Jesus in bodily form, forever triumphant over sin and death, offering resurrection life to all who will come to Him.

CHARACTER WITNESSES

The final evidence of the truthfulness of the Christian faith is that Jesus Christ changes lives. He did it in the first century; He is doing it today. The fact that Jesus Christ changes lives does not, by itself, make Christianity true. There are many people who can point to a changed life through a religious encounter which is non-Christian. However, if Christianity is the true God-given faith, then we would expect it to change lives. We have already shown sufficient evidence for one to believe that Christianity is true intellectually. Now we will show that a personal commitment to Jesus Christ dramatically changes the believers life for the better.

The Disciples Of Jesus

The disciples of Jesus were His constant companions for three years, staying with Him through very difficult times. However, after His betrayal by Judas Iscariot they all left Him. Simon Peter denied even knowing Him. At Jesus' trial none of them stood up for Him. At His crucifixion they were silent and motionless. Yet less than two months after His crucifixion these same cowardly men were boldly proclaiming to the world that Jesus had risen. Nearly every one of them went through terrible persecution and eventually died a martyr's death.

Something happened to change these men from cowards into martyrs. The fact that their lives were changed is not in dispute. The big question is, "What changed them?" They said it was seeing the risen Christ and then committing their lives to Him. The changed lives of the disciples testify to the fact of the truthfulness of the Christian faith.

Saul Of Tarsus

Another example of a changed life is that of Saul of Tarsus. The great persecutor of Christians became their main advocate. It is an undisputed fact that Saul was a changed man. He went from despising the name of Jesus to worshiping the name of Jesus. He went from a hater of Christians to become the greatest missionary in the history of the church. Something changed his life. Saul testified it was meeting the risen Christ. Along with the testimony of the disciples, Saul's conversion gives evidence to the truthfulness of the Christian faith.

Millions More

The disciples of Jesus and Saul of Tarsus are not the only ones who Jesus Christ has touched and changed. Literally millions of people throughout history have their lives changed through meeting the risen Christ. Theologian E. Y. Mullins wrote, "I have, for me at least, irrefutable evidence of the objective existence of the Person so moving me. When to this personal experience I add that tens of thousands of living Christians, and an unbroken line of them back to Christ, and when I find in the New Testament a manifold record of like experiences, together with a clear account of the origin and cause of them all, my certainty becomes absolute" (E. Y. Mullins, *Why Is Christianity True?* Chicago: Christian Culture Press, 1905, pp. 284, 285).

Christianity not only offers irrefutable evidence of being true, it also passes the personal test. It is the only faith that can ultimately satisfy the individual. It changes our lives, heals our broken hearts and gives us peace in the midst of turmoil. Christian experience verifies the truth of the Christian faith.

Weighing The Evidence

WEIGHING THE EVIDENCE

In spite of all the evidence and the promises of changed lives, some people are still reluctant to accept Jesus Christ as their personal Lord and Savior. Are you one of the reluctant ones? If so, your reason(s) for holding back are probably among those below. See if one or more of these expresses your concerns.

Objection One: "I don't need it— Christianity is just a crutch."

"Life is fine the way it is. I have no need of anything. I can stand on my own two feet. I don't need Jesus Christ." However, we all need Jesus. God is not a luxury He is a necessity. You may feel fulfilled in your present lifestyle, but that satisfaction is at best only temporary. Jesus said:, "For what advantage is it to a man if he gains the whole world, and is himself destroyed or lost?" (Luke 9:25).

You may have everything material and emotional in this life, yet you may lack the most important thing of all, knowing God personally through Jesus Christ. Maybe you do not have a lot of earthly possessions, but you still have peace of mind in your simple lifestyle. That's fine. You still need Jesus Christ. If you feel Christianity is just a crutch, it must be said that all of us use one kind of crutch or another to get by. Admitting the need for Jesus is not a sign of weakness; it is a sign of wisdom.

Objection Two: "Too many hypocrites."

One common excuse that is used to reject the Christian faith concerns the number of hypocrites in the church. A hypocrite is an actor, a person who puts on a false face. He says one thing, yet he does something else. Examples of hypocrisy, both past and present, are readily pointed to, many of which involve people in the ministry. This supposedly invalidates the Christian faith.

Yes, there are people today who go to church and are hypocrites. Their lives are inconsistent with what they say they believe. This, however, does not invalidate Christianity. It just demonstrates that some people who claim to be Christians are hypocrites. For every example of a hypocrite, a counter-example of someone living consistently with his Christian beliefs can be observed.

Part of the problem is the failure to distinguish between hypocrisy and sin. All Christians are sinners but they are not all hypocrites. A person becomes a Christian by admitting he is a sinner and with God's help he tries to keep from sinning. Jesus had some very strong words for those who were practicing religious hypocrisy: "But woe to you, scribes and Pharisees, hypocrites! For you shut up the kingdom of heaven against men; for you neither go in yourselves, nor do you allow those who are entering to go in. Woe to you, scribes and Pharisees, hypocrites! For you devour widows houses, and for a pretense make long prayers. Therefore you will receive greater condemnation" (Matthew 23:13,14).

Objection Three: "I'm already good enough."

Why should I become a Christian—I'm already good enough to go to heaven. I've never killed anyone, I've lived a decent life. If there is a heaven, I certainly deserve to go there. This view misses what the Bible says about a person's relationship to God and heaven and how to get there. The Bible clearly says, in many places, that good works are not credits toward heaven. Jesus' disciples asked Him what kind of works would get them approval from God: "Then they said to Him, 'What shall we do, that we may work the works of God?' Jesus answered and said to them, 'This is the work of God, that you believe in Him whom He sent" (John 6:28, 29).

"For by grace you have been saved through faith, and that not of yourselves; it is the gift of God, not of works, lest anyone should boast" (Ephesians 2:8,9).

I hope that you're not trusting in your good works to get to heaven. None of us, no matter how good, can make it on our own.

Objection Four: "I'm not good enough yet."

"I'm not good enough now to be a Christian—I still have some bad habits. But when I stop doing these things, then I'll be good enough to be a Christian."

Unfortunately, a lot of people hold the view that being a Christian is the same as being a good person. They observe their lives and see some habits that are not consistent with what they think a

Christian should be and think that only when they change their lifestyle can they become a Christian. This involves two misconceptions. First, a Christian is not a "good" person. A Christian is someone who is a sinner and who has admitted that fact, and has asked God for forgiveness. Second, no one can or ever will be good enough to be a Christian. Merely breaking a few bad habits does not make a person acceptable to God. God's standard is one of perfection. The only way to approach God is through His Son, Jesus Christ. "For there is one God and one Mediator between God and men, the Man Christ Jesus" (1 Timothy 2:5).

Objection Five: "I'll never be good enough."

Another excuse people use to keep from becoming a Christian is that they will never be good enough. They feel that their lives have been so ruined that God could never forgive them. Others believe that they do not have the ability to be a Christian or live the Christian life. They mistakenly think God doesn't want them. Fortunately, there is good news for both types of people. No matter how bad you have been, no matter how much you have ruined your life, there is still forgiveness available. Jesus Christ said, "Come to Me, all you who labor and are heavy laden, and I will give you rest" (Matthew 11:28). "All that the Father gives Me will come to Me, and the one who comes to Me I will by no means cast out" (John 6:37). What great news! You have not passed the point of no return. God can and will forgive you if you ask Him.

There is also good news for those who do not feel they have the ability to live the Christian life. The Christian life is not a difficult life to live—it is an impossible life to live. You cannot do it. It must be lived through us by the power of the Holy Spirit, who indwells each believer. It is God working through us who makes it possible.

Objection Six: "Maybe someday I'll believe, but not now."

Whatever the excuse may be, these people are not yet ready to become Christians. The problem is that tomorrow never comes. We all believe we will live a long life but which of us can say how long we will live? Jesus gave the following parable: "The ground of a certain rich man yielded plentifully. And he thought within himself, saying, 'What shall I do, since I have no room to store my crops?' So he said, 'I will do this: I will pull down my barns and build greater, and there I will store all my crops and my goods. And I will say to my soul, Soul you have many goods laid up for many years; take your ease; eat, drink, and be merry.' But God said to him, 'You fool! This night your soul will be required of you; then whose will those things be which you have provided? So is he who lays up treasure for himself, and is not rich toward God" (Luke 12:16-21).

We do not know when it will be our time to die. The Bible encourages us to trust Jesus Christ now and not to put it off. Do not wait until the eleventh hour to repent—you might die at ten-thirty!

Objection Seven: "I don't want my life changed."

"My life is fine the way it is." People like these realize that becoming a Christian would mean a changed life. Some people would rather continue in their sins. Jesus said, "And this is the condemnation, that the light has come into the world, men loved darkness rather than light, because their deeds were evil" (John 3:19).

People whose highest goal is to give themselves pleasure are called hedonists. Hedonists will sacrifice anything for their own selfish interests. However, rejecting Jesus Christ to wallow in sin is self-defeating. While securing pleasure for a season, these people are storing up an eternity of judgment and separation from God. Since accepting Jesus Christ is the ultimate satisfaction for any human being, hedonists owe it to themselves to consider Jesus' offer of the free gift of salvation and the genuine joy of a fulfilling abundant life in Christ. Wouldn't it be worth while to think about exchanging the transitory pleasures for an eternity of happiness?

Objection Eight: "I don't want to believe."

When it comes right down to it, many people reject Christ simply because they don't want to believe. It is not that they cannot believe; they will not believe. One of the miracles Jesus performed was raising a man named Lazarus from the dead. The religious leaders who knew of this fact not only wanted to kill Jesus for this, they wanted to kill Lazarus also! They wanted to destroy the evidence! Their unbelief certainly was not because of lack of evidence.

A Christian friend of mine has a radio talk show in which he interviews a variety of guests. He told me that over the years, he has had occasion to interview dozens of atheists, and agnostics. He always asks them the question, "If I could prove to you, to your satisfaction, that Jesus Christ was the Son of God, and that He did come back from the dead, would that make a difference in your attitude toward Him?"

Almost everyone he has asked has said no, it would not make a difference. As with the religious leaders of Jesus' day, these people do not have a problem of the mind, they have a problem of the will. No matter what the facts may be, they refuse to believe.

Objection Nine: "I don't want to be religious."

Many people believe that becoming a Christian involves adapting a restrictive lifestyle. Since this is what their idea of a Christian is, they do not find Christianity appealing. Unfortunately some Christians give this impression. Jesus, however, said that He had come that we might have life abundantly (John 10:10). Rather than being a dull, boring life, the Christian experience is one of adventure and fulfillment. It's exciting being a Christian! We have the freedom to be the person God created us to be. While it is true there are certain things God commands us not to do, these commandments are for our own good.

Religious? No. Boring? No. Exciting? Yes! That's what being a Christian is all about. Jesus said, "Therefore if the Son makes you free, you will be free indeed" (John 8:36).

Objection Ten: "What would my friends think?"

"If I become a Christian, I would lose my job my wife would leave me, my friends would think I'm crazy." This excuse is common, but it is not valid. We're always afraid of how the other person is going to view what we are going to do. People might think we've gone off the deep end. We don't want to risk that, so we remain in our secure position, even though we know it isn't right. Any division caused by serving Jesus Christ is based upon who is following the truth and who is not. Jesus made it clear that those who follow Him are seeking the truth: "I am the way, the truth and the life. No one comes to the Father except through Me" (John 14:6).

What kind of friend is it who rejects you because you find peace, joy and satisfaction? A real friend will be happy for you. The Bible makes it clear who your real friend is: His name is Jesus: "For when we were still without strength, in due time Christ died for the ungodly. For scarcely for a righteous man will one die; yet perhaps for a good man someone would even dare to die. But God demonstrates His own love toward us, in that while we were still sinners, Christ died for us" (Romans 5:6-8).

Objection Eleven: "I don't understand the issue."

Sometimes people do not become Christians because they do not understand what it is all about. The ignorance can be self-imposed or merely a lack of information on the subject. Self-imposed ignorance about Jesus Christ is common. People do not know about Jesus because they do not want to be responsible to Him. Moreover, the Bible teaches that this ignorance is something which the unbeliever is actively participating:

"For the wrath of God is revealed from heaven against all ungodliness and unrighteousness of men, who suppress the truth in unrighteousness" (Romans 1:18).

There is another type of ignorance where people are unaware that it is possible to have a personal relationship with God through Jesus Christ. They think Christianity is just another religion, practiced by going through the motions. It is a ritual, a set of laws.

Once I was walking along the beach in California with a friend and I asked, "What kept you from becoming a Christian for so long?" My friend replied, "Nobody ever told me that I could know God in a personal way. I did not know that Jesus cared for me and wanted to have a personal relationship with me." There are many who are still unaware of God's gift of salvation.

Objection Twelve: "It's not relevant."

"This is the twentieth century. How can someone who lived two thousand years ago have any affect on my life today?" People feel they have more important things to do then worry about the identity of Jesus. However, nothing could be further from the truth. If Jesus Christ is the Lord of the universe, and if eternal happiness and peace with God is only available through a personal relationship with Him, then there is nothing more relevant to your entire existence. It does matter.

The Verdict

THE VERDICT

You are the judge. You have been presented with the best possible evidence. You know the facts. You know the importance of this case. You know that the Bible is an accurate historical record. You know that Jesus Christ proved He was God in human flesh. You know that the abundant life from Jesus includes peace between you and God, you and other people, you and the world and even between you and yourself.

Against a world that sees man as a chance product of evolutionary forces, a cosmic accident, the Bible tells us we have been made in the image and likeness of God. We are not animals. We are personal beings with the capacity for love, free will and interpersonal relationships. We are created to know and love God, to be fulfilled in Him. In today's world people are desperately searching for someone to give them meaning to life and death issues. Jesus Christ is the only one who can give real meaning to the questions of existence beyond the grave. Death is not the "great escape" or the "last sleep." Because of Jesus' triumph over death, His resurrection from the dead, those who love Him need never fear death. It becomes a transition from this world to the heavenly world of eternal peace with God.

God has given us sufficient evidence. Jesus Christ is waiting for your verdict. You are the judge. You have everything to gain by ruling in your favor and for the lordship of Jesus Christ. Hand down your verdict now and turn your life over to Jesus. He cares! You'll never be sorry. There is a life hanging in the balance in this "case"— yours. Let it be a life given to Jesus Christ. If you would like to become a Christian right now, pray a simple prayer like this:

Lord Jesus, I know that I'm a sinner. Thank you for dying for me.
Right this moment, in the best way that I know how, I trust You as my own Savior and Lord. Thank you Lord, for saving me.
In Jesus' Name, Amen.

If you just prayed this prayer, congratulations! You have decided for Jesus Christ and for eternal life.

In doing so you have established this day as your spiritual birthday, and I would like to know about it. Please take a moment to write me at: Box 6486, Orange, California, 92613. God Bless You!

Don Stewart is one of the most successful writers in the country having authored or co-authored over thirty books. These include: *10 Reasons to Trust the Bible; The Bible and Science: Are They in Conflict?* and *What Everyone Needs To Know About Jesus.*

His writings have also achieved international success. Thirty of his titles have been translated into different languages including Chinese, Finnish, Polish, Spanish, German, and Portuguese.

He received his undergraduate degree at Biola University majoring in Bible. He received a masters degree from Talbot Theological Seminary graduating with the highest honors and he is a member of the national honor society, Kappa Tau Epsilon.

Don is also an internationally known apologist, a defender of the historic Christian faith. In his defense of Christianity he has traveled to over thirty countries speaking at colleges, universities, churches, seminars, and retreats. His topics include: the evidence for Christianity, the identity of Jesus Christ, the challenge of the cults, and the relationship of the Bible and science.

Other Books By Don Stewart

10 Reasons to Trust the Bible $6.95

The Coming Temple:
Center Stage for the Final Countdown
                                          $9.95
In Search of the Lost Ark:
The Quest for the Ark of the Covenant
                                         $11.95

Basic Bible Study Series ($9.95 each)

What Everyone Needs to Know About God

What Everyone Needs to Know About
Jesus

What Everyone Needs to Know About the
Holy Spirit

What Everyone Needs to Know About the
Bible

Please add $2.00 for shipping and
handling. California residents
add 7.75 % sales tax.

AusAmerica Publishers
Box 6486
Orange, California 92613

**To order books by credit card
call toll free
1-800-637-5177**